New Orleans
An Artist's Sketchbook

original pen & ink drawings by
Steven Lindsley

text by
Tom Horner

TRYON PUBLISHING COMPANY, INC.
CHAPEL HILL

ACKNOWLEDGEMENTS

The editors, the artist, and the author would like to thank Dr. W. Kenneth Holditch, Research Professor of English at the University of New Orleans, and Dr. Jon Kukla, Director of the Historic New Orleans Collection, for reading the manuscript and making valuable suggestions and corrections.

I would also like to express thanks to Pamela Arceneaux and the staff of the Historic New Orleans Collection for their kind assistance to me personally and to the New Orleans Arts Council for suggesting Steven Lindsley to do the drawings for this book. Thanks also to Judy Lanier for her major contributions in research and editorial assistance.

—*Tom Horner*

Cover is based upon the Serigny view of New Orleans in 1719,
from reproduction in J. Winsor, *Narrative and critical history of America,* V. 39,
of an inset in M. de Serigny's 'Carte de la Cote de la Louisiane en 1719 et 1720'.

Printed in the United States of America

ISBN 1-884824-03-X

New Orleans
An Artist's Sketchbook

TABLE OF CONTENTS

INTRODUCTION

New Orleans' most distinctive aspect is a varied heritage with strong reflections of its French and Spanish background. Just as a European princess, through a series of arranged marriages, was often the pawn in the game of political alliances, Louisiana with her crown jewel New Orleans was ceded back and forth among the world's powers. Rather than losing her identity through many transitions, she garnered special characteristics from each of her ruling countries, emerging finally with a personality wholly in tact and distinct from any North American city.

In 1682 the French Canadian explorer LaSalle proclaimed the Mississippi Valley for Louis XIV, King of France, and in 1718 another French Canadian, Sieur de Bienville, founded a city, naming it for Louis' nephew, the Duke of Orleans. Had the French not founded New Orleans at that time, both the Spanish and the English were waiting on the sidelines to do so, and would have claimed Louisiana as well.

The treaty that ended the French and Indian War in 1763 ceded Louisiana to Spain. In November 1803 the Spanish flag was replaced in Place D'Armes (Jackson Square) and the French flag waved once again. Three weeks later the American flag was raised there. Napoleon, having just received the territory from Spain, sold it to the United States in the great Louisiana Purchase.

Though the city remained strongly culturally French, the Spanish were not without considerable influence. Because of two disastrous fires during the Spanish period (in 1788 and 1794) most of the buildings were burned. Those rebuilt were Spanish, and the Spanish had enacted a new code — all buildings of three stories had to be built of brick. One story structures could be of wood. After 1803, the code was followed only sporadically, but the general uniformity of height pervaded. Walk through the French Quarter and notice the distance from the sidewalk to the top of the highest buildings and note how this forms a pleasant view when looking down any street. Unlike the views between the skyscrapers of many major American cities, the streets of the French quarter are pleasing to the eye and restful to the soul.

The French settlers, now blended with the Spanish, were called Creoles. Immigrants from the American states were simply 'les

Americains.' Those who prospered built stately mansions on St. Charles Avenue in the Garden District, so named for its beautiful exterior gardens, which contrasted with the center court gardens typifying the French Quarter.

An even greater influence than 'les Americains' were African slaves, free blacks, and immigrants from Haiti. They brought to New Orleans the shotgun house, gumbo, red beans and rice, and a distinctive music. Native Americans continued to wield considerable influence on the cultural development of New Orleans well into the eighteenth century. Their strong craft tradition survives today.

The Civil War liberated the slaves and helped to heal the former enmity between Creoles and Americans. The city prospered, becoming America's largest port. In 1884 it celebrated a centennial of cotton exportation with a world's fair in Audubon Park and a century later held a second world's fair at the Riverwalk.

Horse racing emerged as a popular pastime early in the nineteenth century, and many tracks thrived until the Civil War. In 1872, following the end of the War, a track was built at the Fair Grounds off Esplanade Avenue which is still in use today, making it the third oldest in America, after Saratoga and Pimlico. Mardi Gras and its parades have been a part of the city's life since 1837. This finale of Carnival season has become New Orleans' largest annual festival. JazzFest, held later in the Spring, has grown into the city's second largest celebration. On two successive weekends in April, it is held at the Fair Grounds with events taking place throughout the city on intervening days.

Along with the racing and revelry, New Orleans has nurtured music, literature and art. One of her major contribution's to this country's culture has been a truly American art form -- jazz.

New Orleans is ever changing and ever the same: the European princess, the ageless beauty, America's only Mediterranean city. Unique among cities, New Orleans rolls on, like the mighty river on whose banks she stands.

— *Tom Horner*

New Orleans
An Artist's Sketchbook

LaSalle

Native Americans of the Louisiana region had developed a highly organized society as early as 700 BC. The rich Mississippi Delta was a natural center for hunting and farming and by 1700 as many as 15,000 people inhabited the region which now comprises Louisiana -- the Caddo, Natchez, Atakapa, Chitimachan, Tunican and the Muskogean. Major among these tribes were the Caddo, numbering about 8,000, whose members dwelled in conical, grass-thatched homes and hunted, fished and farmed.

Louisiana became a blend of many ingredients. Early Spanish explorers, among them Hernando de Soto, explored the Mississippi River Valley, claiming much of the area for Spain in 1541. Left largely untouched and raw, the Mississippi Valley, named "father of the waters" by the Indians, was relatively ignored by Europeans for about 150 years.

In 1682, a French explorer from Montreal, Robert Cavalier, Sieur de LaSalle, traveled down the Mississippi from the Great Lakes in Canada, reaching the mouth of the Mississippi in April of that year. LaSalle claimed the entire Mississippi Valley for France on April 9, 1681, and named it Louisiana for the King of France, Louis XIV, "the Sun King."

The French hoped to gain control of fur trading from the American interior, but growth of the colony progressed slowly as France was engaged in war in Europe and was short of funds to seed further development. Even private companies failed to promote colonization, and by 1750 there were only approximately 10,000 European settlers in the area.

In 1762, after 80 years of French rule, the territory west of the Mississippi was ceded to Spain and remained under Spanish control for the next forty years.

This interpretation of LaSalle's declaration is based on an old print in the Chicago Historical Society collection.

⚜

In 1718, seeking a location to establish a desirable settlement and secure the Mississippi River and Louisiana against Spain and England, Jean Baptist LeMoyne, Sieur de Bienville, governor of the French colony of Louisiana, founded New Orleans on a more or less dry stretch of land near the river, about 100 miles from the Gulf of Mexico. The city was named for the Regent of France, Phillippe Duc d'Orleans.

The city's founding has since been commemorated in this statuary grouping of Bienville, an Indian and Father Anthanase Douay, the Bienville expedition's guide. The work of sculptor Angela Gregory, the 26-foot, two

Łindsley

ton statue was erected in front of Union Station in 1955. It recently found a new home in a small triangular park at the intersection of Decatur, Conti, and North Peters Streets in the French Quarter.

Nicknamed the Crescent City because of its location on an enormous sweeping curve of the Mississippi, the city has fought a constant battle with the environment. Levees were raised and much of the swampy terrain was filled with oyster shells and cypress pilings.

France widely promoted the colony, and young adventurers arrived to help the city take shape. The Creole culture was born of the city's French and Spanish families who had intermarried for decades; thus, when Spain regained control of the territory in 1762, New Orleans remained virtually the same.

Madame John's Legacy, 632 Dumaine Street, is a raised basement, single story home located in the city's French Quarter. Originally built in 1726 or 1727 by Jean Pascal, a ship's captain from Provence, the one story structure was apparently moved a short distance and placed on top of a brick basement sometime in 1788. The house has a deep front porch with seven wooden columns and wood railings. Doors from the basement floor open onto the street and two dormers adorn the roof. A rear gallery contains simple windows and doors of the early French design. Some believe the house is the oldest building in the Mississippi Valley, though this claim is contested by the Ursuline Convent.

Untouched by the first great fire in New Orleans, the house changed hands several times before being purchased by a Mrs. I.I. Lehmann in the 1920s. The house is currently owned by the Louisiana State Museum system, but is not open to the public.

The name, "Madame John's Legacy," comes from a short story, "'Tite Poulette," written by George Washington Cable in 1879. In the story a man named John left his house to his quadroon mistress Zalli, or Madame John, and 'Tite Poulette, Zalli's daughter. The legacy came to naught when Zalli sold the house and put the money in a bank which then failed.

The Ursuline Convent, located at 1141 Chartres, is reputed to be the oldest European built structure in the Mississippi Valley; the original structure was erected in 1734. In the early eighteenth century, the Ursulines of France, known as the "Gray Sisters," contracted to educate the young in Louisiana, and in 1726 a band of nuns and postulants set out for the New World. Their journey was chronicled by a young novice named Madeleine Hachard, who left her family on the adventure of a lifetime, never to return to her native country.

The nuns traveled by stagecoach to the French coast, and along the way were considered objects of interest as local townspeople lined the roads to catch a glimpse of them. At the ship, the *Gironde*, no gangplank was available so a thoughtful ship's captain arranged to have the women hoisted aboard individually in an armchair to preserve their modesty. The group was accompanied by a small cat which had taken up with them somewhere along the way. Their cabin was tiny, only eighteen feet by seven feet, with three tiers of bunks, so close together that they could not sit up. So stuffy was the atmosphere below decks that the sisters elected to use the room in shifts. The voyage to the mouth of the Mississippi took five long months, during which time the nuns were given up for dead. They suffered through storms, were threatened by pirates and were entreated to stay in Santo Domingo by plantation owners there. During their final leg of the journey to New Orleans they traveled by pirogues, or dugout canoes, slept on the ground, and suffered from exposure to rain, mosquitoes, colds and what was termed "more considerable malady," probably diarrhea.

In her journals and correspondence, Madeleine described New Orleans as "very beautiful, finely constructed and regularly built," although about the people she stated there was "not one devout person in all the country." Certainly, the Ursulines had their work cut out for them. And work they did, starting immediately to educate the girls of New Orleans, taking in boarding pupils as well as day students, and starting classes for black and Indian girls. In addition, officials wanted them to assume charge of "girls of bad conduct," both local and those sent from France. They also took in the "casket girls," early imported brides so called because of the chests or "caskets" of clothing which were provided by the king of France.

The convent itself, which took seven years to complete, was considered to be a sizeable construction project for its time. The entire facility sprawls over half a city block, a brick plastered two and one-half story building constructed in the French Renaissance style. The convent is a rich, elegant structure, with iron grills protecting the first floor windows and blue-green shutters to batten the windows on the second floor. Dormers were evenly spaced in the sloping tile roof. The interior was quite plain as bespoke the traditions of the Ursulines. Major Amos Stoddard described the convent in 1812 thusly: "It will accommodate about fifty nuns and from seventy to eighty young females who resort to it for their education. Attached to the Convent is a small house containing three rooms divided by double gratings six inches asunder with apertures two inches square where strangers may see and converse with the nuns and boarders on particular business." A series of outbuildings included classrooms, a laundry, chapel and barns, and the property contained vegetable plots and gardens as well.

In 1824 the nuns sold the convent and moved elsewhere. Today it houses archives and records of the archdiocese of New Orleans, but it is still known as the old convent, and stands, a little worn to be sure, stately and graceful, a legacy to the city from the "Gray Sisters." Adjacent is St. Mary's Italian Church which was built in 1845.

And what of Madeleine Hachard? She devoted thirty-five years of her life to the Ursulines, becoming known for her ceaseless energy and her smile. In August of 1760, missed at Mass, she was found in her tiny cell, "sleeping the long sleep of death."

⚜

Lafitte's Blacksmith Shop, located at 941 Bourbon Street, was owned by the brother of pirate Jean Lafitte, and was built in the early 1770s. Lafitte was an iron mason and it is possible, although no evidence exists to support this, that the infamous outlaw used the blacksmith shop as a front for some of his illegal operations. Now housing a bar, the shop was originally built as a small house. In spots, the stucco overlay is worn and the original "briquette-entre-poteaux" construction can be seen.

Jean Lafitte and his brother Pierre were hunted by the American government for acts of piracy and smuggling during the early seventeenth century. Though patronized by the wealthy and aided and abetted by the common folk, the pirates and their ilk were nonetheless considered criminals, and Jean Lafitte was among the most notable of the time. When Governor Claiborne put a five hundred dollar reward on his head, Lafitte arrogantly countered with a fifteen hundred dollar bounty for the governor! In 1814, during what was known as the War of 1812, New Orleans was under siege by the British, who offered to purchase the pirates' loyalties. Negotiating through New Orleans businessman Jean Blanque, the pirates, headed by Lafitte, offered to fight on the side of the Americans in return for a pardon. The pardon was granted, and the pirates' contribution of men and armament helped General Andrew Jackson's army defeat the British. Jean Lafitte, pirate, smuggler, defender of New Orleans, died in 1826.

The national park at the site of the battle in Chalmette is named in his honor.

LaFitte's Blacksmith Shop

The Cathedral of Saint Louis, patron saint of France, towers over Jackson Square, formerly called the Place d'Armes. A church building has stood on this site since the very earliest days of New Orleans. The first church met its end in 1722 in a hurricane; the second was destroyed by fire in 1788. Don Almonester y Roxas, builder of the Cabildo and the Presbytere, erected the present Cathedral, stipulating that upon his death, the congregation should pray for his soul.

Early plans for the Cathedral clearly show that the architect had the Cabildo and the Presbytere in mind when he designed the church, designing it without spires to keep the buildings in harmony with one another. The structure was completed in 1794 and bell-shaped turrets were added to the towers in 1814, along with granite fir-cones to ornament the parapet. Of interest to historians is that St. Anthony's Garden behind the church was once a notorious dueling ground.

Almonester was made a Knight of the Order of Charles III in 1796, but was only able to enjoy this distinction for two years, dying in 1798 at the age of seventy-three. His body was first buried in the parish churchyard but was later brought inside the cathedral and buried beneath its marble floor. A tablet listing the don's many good works rests on the site.

To the outrage of modern architectural critics, the Cathedral, which had fallen into disrepair, was remodeled in 1851. Then city surveyor, Louis Pilie, redesigned the facade of the cathedral after the collapse of one of the towers. He gave it a more classical portico and replaced the bell towers with steeples, which were in architectural vogue at the time.

The Cathedral is home to the oldest church congregation in the Mississippi Valley and is the oldest Catholic cathedral in America. The Cathedral is pictured here through the front gates of Jackson Square.

The Historic New Orleans Collection, founded by General and Mrs. L. Kemper Williams, is housed at 527-533 Royal Street, which is the location of the 1792 Merieult House and also the elegant "hidden house" residence of the founders. The Merieult House was built in 1792 by merchant Jean Francois Merieult.

From the large courtyard of the structure, long stairways lead to the second floor gallery, which has railings of unusually simple design. The Williams residence is furnished in various periods and shows the opulence of New Orleans during the mid-twentieth century.

The Collection complex includes the Merieult House, the Counting

The Cathedral of St. Louis

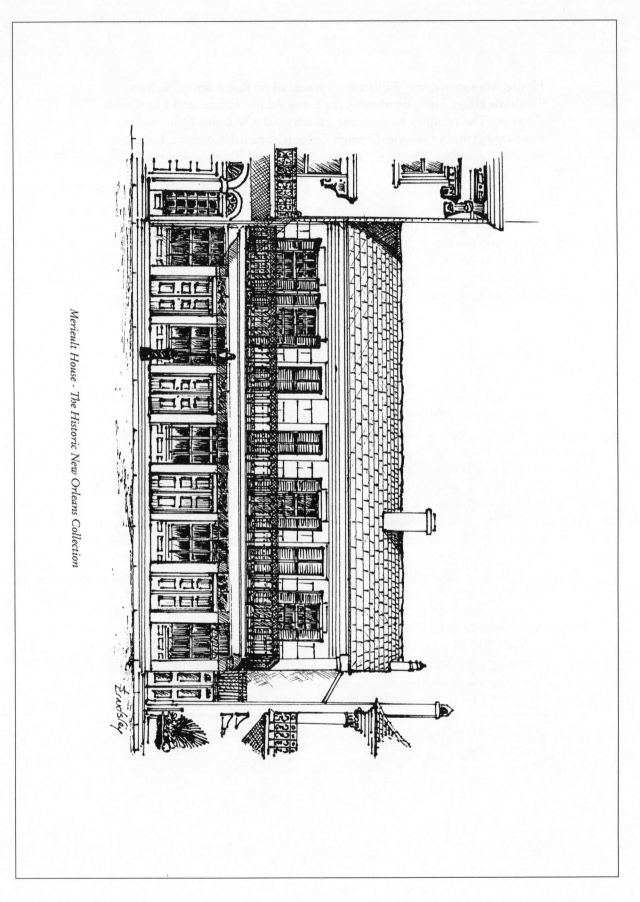

House, Maisonette, the Williams residence, all on Royal Street; and on Toulouse Street The Townhouse, the Louis Adams House, and The Creole Cottage. The complex houses nine galleries : the Williams Gallery; the Louisiana History Galleries (French Colonial, Spanish Colonial, Louisiana Purchase, Empire, Victorian, Decorative Arts, and Plantation); and the River Gallery.

The Collection includes priceless documents pertaining to the Louisiana Purchase of 1803 and to the Federal Occupation of New Orleans during the Civil War. Special exhibits highlight Mardi Gras, the arts, New Orleans cuisine and the city's cultural diversity. On display is the only portrait of Bienville to be found in North America. This valuable collection is indispensable for those who want to research the history of the city and the early colony of Louisiana.

⚜

The Cabildo, also referred to as the Casa Capitular or Government House, on St. Peter Street next to the Cathedral on Jackson Square, was built in 1795-97 as the executive offices for the Spanish governor. It was designed and constructed by Don Almonester y Roxas, the Spanish businessman who, though widely disliked, grew to be a wealthy and generous benefactor in New Orleans. He used his wealth and promises to build a church and a hospital in order to buy himself a government appointment as "alcalde."

The Cabildo replaced the government building on the same site which was destroyed in the second great fire in the city's history. Don Almonester was not only the contractor and builder, he was also the lender of funds required to build the facility, thus ensuring his continued position of importance in the town. One of the most outstanding examples of Spanish architecture in New Orleans, the Cabildo is a solid mass of stuccoed brick with large columns and wrought-iron balconies.

Within its walls, some of the negotiations for the Louisiana Purchase were conducted by Governor William Claiborne, and the American flag first flew over its balcony in 1803. It served as the City Hall until 1858 and in 1861, when Louisiana seceded from the Union, the Cabildo became the location for Confederate offices. The Cabildo suffered serious fire damage in 1988 and has undergone extensive restoration. It is owned by the Louisiana State Museum.

The Cabildo

The Presbytere

The Presbytere is located on Jackson Square and flanks the Cathedral of St. Louis on one side, as its companion structure, the Cabildo, does on the other. Also designed by Don Andres Almonester y Roxas, the Presbytere is nearly identical in structure to the Cabildo; it was built in stages from 1794 to 1847. The construction that started in 1794 on the Presbytere, which was intended as a church house or rectory, was interrupted first by Almonester's disagreements with the resident Capuchin monks, and then by the more important construction of the Cabildo. The Presbytere was never used as a rectory but as a city courthouse and is today a part of the Louisiana State Museum, having been acquired by the city in 1853. The Louisiana Portrait Gallery and exhibits about the history and culture of the state are among the displays currently found in the Presbytere.

The Presbytere, together with the Cabildo, the Cathedral, and the Pontalba Apartments, constitute one of the most elegant public squares in the country.

⚜

Late in 1803, Louisiana reverted to French rule, with the condition that the territory never be ceded to another power. The local population was jubilant. A short time later, Napoleon sold the entire territory to the United States for $15 million. A portion of the treaty which became known as "The Louisiana Purchase" is reproduced on the following page. Not only did France's agreement with Spain forbid such a transaction, Napoleon made the agreement without consulting his legislature and the United States Constitution had no provisions for such a purchase. In December of that year, the American flag was ceremoniously raised in the Place D'Armes, now known as Jackson Square, with the Cabildo standing serenely in the background as rifles fired a salute.

Americans, who were considered uncivilized, crude backwoodsmen by the Creoles, poured into the city bringing with them a new culture along with substantial wealth and investment capital, a fact that soon quieted the cultural friction.

Geographically, the Americans created their own neighborhoods, among them the famous Garden District, and architectural designs took a more Classical turn. Canal Street divides the French Quarter and the more "American" portion of the city.

When Louisiana attained statehood in 1812, New Orleans became an American city officially, though in spirit, it remained a world to itself.

Treaty Between the United States of America and the French Republic

The President of the United States of America, and the First Consul of the French Republic, in the name of the French people, desiring to remove all source of misunderstanding, relative to objects of discussion mentioned in the second and fifth articles of the Convention of . . . September 30, 1800, relative to the rights claimed by the United States, in virtue of the treaty concluded at Madrid, the 27th of October, 1795, between His Catholic Majesty and the said United States, and willing to strengthen the union and friendship, which at the time of the said Convention was happily reestablished between the two nations, have respectively named their Plenipotentiaries, to wit: The President of the United States of America, by and with the advice and consent of the Senate of the said States, Robert R. Livingston, Minister Plenipotentiary of the United States, and James Monroe, Minister Plenipotentiary and Envoy Extraordinary of the said States, near the Government of the French Republic; and the First Consul, in the name of the French people, the French citizen Barbé-Marbois, Minister of the Public Treasury, who, after having respectively exchanged their full powers, have agreed to the following articles:

Art. 1. Whereas, by the article the third of the Treaty concluded at St. Ildefonso October 1, 1800, between the First Consul of the French Republic and His Catholic Majesty (of Spain), it was agreed as follows: His Catholic Majesty promises and engages on his part to cede to the French Republic, six months after the full and entire execution of the conditions and stipulations herein, relative to His Royal Highness the Duke of Parma, the Colony or Province of Louisiana, ...: And whereas, in pursuance of the Treaty, particularly of the third article, the French Republic has an incontestible title to the domain and to the possession of the said territory, the First Consul of the French Republic, desiring to give to the United States a strong proof of friendship, doth hereby cede to the said United States, in the name of the French Republic, forever and in full sovereignty, the said territory, with all its rights and appurtenances, as fully and in the same manner as they might have been acquired by the French Republic, in value of the above-mentioned treaty, concluded with His Catholic Majesty.

In faith whereof, the respective Plenipotentiaries have signed these articles in the French and English languages, declaring, nevertheless, that the present treaty was originally agreed to in the French language, and have thereunto put their seals.

Done at Paris, the 10th day of Floreal, in the 11th year of the French Republic, and the 30th April, 1803.

R.R. LIVINGSTON,
JAMES MONROE,
BARBÉ-MARBOIS

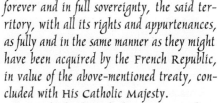

Raising the American flag at Place D'Armes.
Based on a painting at the Cabildo.

Destrehan, owned by the River Road Historical Society, is a few miles from New Orleans and may be reached by the River Road which is also the locale of many other plantation houses. Built in 1797 by Robert Antoine Robin de Logny, it is the oldest plantation house in the lower Mississippi Valley.

In 1802 de Logny's son-in-law, Jean Noel Destrehan de Beaupre, purchased the plantation and over the years accumulated adjacent property, enlarging the holdings considerably. The property remained in the Destrehan family for over one hundred years until it was sold in 1910. Among many notable figures, their guests included the Duke of Orleans, future king of France and pirate Jean LaFitte.

Principal crops of coastal plantations along the Gulf, as well as the Southeastern seaboard, were rice and indigo. As new developments were made in the processing of sugarcane, many large farmers devoted more and more acreage to cane fields, eventually making it their major crop. This proved to be a lucrative trade for many aristocratic plantation owners.

Destrehan's first floor of brick and its upper floor of cypress exemplify the influence of the West Indies on area architecture. New Orleans was not only a close port of entry for the islands and those coming to visit or settle in the area, but similar in climate and environment. It was only natural for architectural features shared with the Indies to emerge in and around the city.

Through local efforts, Destrehan has joined other historic plantations as it has begun exploring the history of its slave population. Though no slave quarters remain on the grounds, the plantation has a rich African-American heritage.

⚜

The house at the corner of Chartres and Saint Louis was once the residence of Nicholas Girod, mayor of New Orleans. The larger three-story section of the house was built in 1814 for Girod, though earlier parts of the structure date to the 1790s. It is supposed that in 1821, Napoleon's sixth year of exile, Girod along with Dominique You, Captain Bossiere, and other supporters of Napoleon planned to rescue the Emperor from St. Helena and bring him to New Orleans.

Whether Girod intended to donate his own house to the Emperor or, as other authorities believe, the house built at 124 Chartres was to be used, the plan failed to come to fruition, as the group learned of Napoleon's death just prior to his setting sail from his island exile.

Napoleon's death mask, now on display in the Presbytere, was brought

Destrehan Plantation

to the city by one of Napoleon's doctors who set up offices in the Girod House when he came to New Orleans.

In the 1920s the Impastato family bought the building and turned the first floor into an eatery that continues to be a favorite with locals and visitors. The Napoleon House Restaurant is, in fact, one of the oldest in the city and is still owned and run by Impastatos. Its mellowed interior is decked with likenesses of the fabled 'emperor' and with images from New Orleans' past. The Napoleon House, together with the recently opened Girod Bistro, provides a spot where casual diners can listen to Mozart and Vivaldi while enjoying historic ambience and charm.

Chalmette Battlefield is part of the Jean LaFitte National Historical Park. Located at 8606 W. St. Bernard Highway, it is exactly six miles below Canal Street in New Orleans. Chalmette is the site of the decisive Battle of New Orleans in which the Americans, under General Andrew Jackson, defeated the British in the War of 1812. Almost every year since 1894, the battle which took place on January 8, 1815 has been commemorated with a large-scale reenactment.

Although the Treaty of Ghent ended the war two weeks before the Battle of New Orleans was fought, this engagement was nonetheless a crucial one. Its importance lay not so much in Jackson's victory, which obviously had no effect on the war's outcome, but in the fact that a defeat would have caused some complex territorial and political problems.

General Sir Edward Pakenham, leader of the British forces, was the brother-in-law of the Duke of Wellington. Wellington had given Pakenham a commission which, should he be victorious, would give him the equivalent authority of a territorial governor "over all the territory fraudulently con-veyed by Bonaparte to the United States." Pakenham was killed in the battle and Wellington, having suffered a series of defeats to American forces, effec-tively abandoned any further ambitions in the former colonies. Jackson's triumph, though late, was considered the greatest of the war and had much to do with his ascendancy to the office of President of the United States.

The battlefield covered an area encompassing five plantations. In 1832, Francois Malus and his brother-in-law Alexandre Le Baron purchased fifteen acres of the original Chalmet Plantation. They designed and built a house for Francois' mother, widow of the great "forgeron" or ironworker Guillaume Malus, whose work includes the balconies of the Napoleon House.

In 1856 Caroline Fabre Cantrelle bought the property and began an extensive renovation which transformed the simple six-room house into a Greek Revival structure with two-story masonry columns. The difficulty of this task has led to speculation that the architect may have been James Gallier, Jr. Further additions were made by subsequent owners Jose Antonio Fernandez y Lineros and Rene Toutant Beauregard, son of Civil War General G.P.T. Beauregard. In 1900, twenty years after Beauregard purchased the house, he added a two-story Victorian wing. The New Orleans Terminal Company owned the house from 1904 until 1949 and during this period the structure fell into terrible disrepair. Under National Park Service ownership the building was remodeled for a visitor's center in 1956-57, effectively saving it from total ruin. Another remodeling in 1993-94 restored the interior to its earlier Greek Revival splendor. The house's role as visitor center has been expanded to include exhibits designed to illustrate downriver plantation culture and architecture.

The Jean Lafitte National Historical Park and Preserve includes the striking Malus-Beauregard House, Chalmette Battlefield, the Chalmette Monument and the Chalmette National Cemetery.

The Beauregard-Keyes House

Located at 1113 Chartres is a home which dates to 1826 or 1827. It was built by Joseph Le Carpentier, grandfather of chess player Paul Morphy, who was born in the house. For a short time (1866-68) it served as the residence of General Pierre Gustave Toutant Beauregard, although for eight years following the Civil War he lived at 934 Royal Street. All in all, Beauregard lived at ten different addresses between 1865 and 1893. In 1889 he purchased the house at 225 Esplanade (now numbered 1631), where he died. However, the home on Chartres Street is the one known as the Beauregard House.

As a young Army engineer in 1849, the Louisiana-born Beauregard was in charge of the construction of the U.S. Custom House on Canal Street. A hero of the Confederacy, Beauregard was the officer who ordered the Confederate bombardment of Fort Sumter, the act which historians credit as igniting the War Between the States.

General Beauregard was a familiar figure in postwar New Orleans. Outsiders observed him as a man of small stature, and were surprised and disappointed in his appearance. But to the people of New Orleans, "the General" was a "Creole imitation of Napoleon," a compact man of erect bearing, the ideal soldier. Active in social and business affairs, the General was a member of several exclusive clubs and organizations.

He was appointed adjutant general of Louisiana in 1879, a post he held for nine years, and in 1888 he was elected Commissioner of Public Works, but resigned after discovering the extensive corruption within the department. Beauregard died on February 20, 1893. His body lay in state in City Hall, guarded by a group of Confederate veterans. He was buried with full military honors in Metairie Cemetery following a procession complete with artillery units, bands and army veterans -- the funeral of a hero.

The novelist Frances Parkinson Keyes lived in the house at 1113 Chartres from 1942 until 1970 and restored both the house and garden to their former glory. Two semicircular staircases leading to the front porch are know as a "welcome staircase." Her books, *Dinner at Antoines* and *Steamboat Gothic* are set in New Orleans.

Today the house is open for tours and features furnishings and memorabilia of both Beauregard and Keyes. The house's design is Neoclassical and is a raised cottage style, similar to that of Madame John's Legacy.

⚜

Located at 1140 Royal Street is what New Orleans terms "the Haunted House." The three story graystone built in the French Empire style is noted for the classic scrollwork of its iron balconies.

Although there is some discrepancy as to when the house was built (various sources indicate anything from 1813 to 1832), it was known to have been the home of Dr. and Mrs. Louis Lalaurie. Madame Lalaurie, the former Marie Delphine MacCarthy, was a beautiful girl, educated in France, who had had two husbands before committing her hand to Dr. Lalaurie. Delphine's mother, Madame MacCarthy, was known to have been a charitable figure in New Orleans society, and was credited with establishing the first school for blacks. Madame MacCarthy was one of the unfortunate victims murdered during a slave uprising early in the nineteenth century, and it has been speculated that this incident may have triggered Delphine's subsequent maltreatment of her slaves.

The most popular legend regarding the house is that while the Lalaurie's were out one evening in 1834, the house caught fire. Neighbors, hearing screams, rushed into the burning house and were appalled to find emaciated slaves chained on the third floor. Of those that died, one was a young girl. The Lalauries were driven out of the city and later fled to France, supposedly never to return, although it was rumored that Mrs. Lalaurie finally came back to this country. In later years, occupants of the house reported hearing strange noises and seeing the apparition of a young girl.

⚜

In 1835, during Andrew Jackson's term as President of the United States, construction began on the first major branch for the United States Mint. Designed by architect William Strickland, the building is a massive three story structure of granite and stuccoed brick located at the corner of Esplanade and Decatur Streets. Like most public buildings in New Orleans it is in the Classic Greek Revival style with the front, which faces Esplanade, boasting an Ionic portico and the rear, a more colorful facade, looking with benign dignity on the busy flea market below.

The mint produced coins with the "O" mintmark from 1838 to about 1862 and returned to operation following the Civil War from 1879 to about 1910. At the beginning of the war, the facility also produced coins for the Confederacy. At its peak, the mint produced about five million dollars in coin each month.

It was at the site of the mint that General Jackson reviewed his troops before their battle against the British and where Confederate William Mumford was hanged for desecrating the American flag during Federal occupation of the building. For a time, the structure served as a Federal prison.

This National Historic Landmark is now a property of the Louisiana State Museum. Exhibits include the Jazz Hall of Fame which features presentations about Bessie Smith and Louis Armstrong. The Mardi Gras exhibit includes costumes, masks, favors and invitations from the past. There is also an exhibit describing the minting process itself. The building houses the Louisiana Historical Center, which maintains important historic documents, manuscripts and newspapers.

The Old United States Mint

After a print in the Historic New Orleans Collection.

The small plain just outside the boundaries of the original walled city has been a gathering place for centuries. It was the site of harvest festivals for Native Americans long before the first European explorers came. From the 1700s onward rhythmic drumbeats, smooth laments, work songs and spirituals filled the air on a small part of that plain known as Congo Square, a place where the Africans of New Orleans could gather on Sundays and hold together their musical and dance traditions. The Square, which is on the National Register of Historic Places, is now part of Louis Armstrong Park, named for the renowned jazz trumpeter and New Orleans native.

Whites who visited Congo Square on Sunday afternoons until the mid 1800s would behold sights which astonished many and which some felt to be immoral. They heard eerie and elemental sounds from a culture much different from their own. By the early days of the 19th century, the black population in New Orleans had increased and most had settled in a section of town far removed from the delicate iron scrollwork seen on Royal Street or in the Garden District. Along the mud-covered road known as "Perdido," meaning "lost," grew a congregation of rickety shanties and shacks which housed many of the city's blacks. Trapped in the bonds of poverty as well as slavery, the city's "people of color" found a way to raise their spirits and soothe their souls. Boxes often served as drums, with bones and sticks used to set the tempos for the chants and the rhythmic, swaying dances that had been passed from generation to generation. These ancient artistic expressions played an elemental role in the beginnings of the New Orleans musical tradition, and ultimately the music and dance traditions of the nation.

Local historians agree that the site of the New Orleans French Market was originally that of a trading post frequented by Indians and fur trappers, and later by German settlers coming downriver to sell vegetables. The market grew and expanded after the Spanish erected a roofed structure on the site in 1791, and tradition holds that it has been open every day since. The present arch is built on the foundations of the original.

In 1806 Governor Claiborne and his Creole wife, the former Clarisse Duralde, would have strolled through the market selecting fish, shrimp, crustaceans, and eggs, and choosing the best from baskets of golden bananas and juicy pineapples. They would have selected from picturesque booths manned by dealers hawking everything from flowers to fowl, turtles to turkeys. Here colorful vendors shouted the wonders of their wares and filled the air with the sounds of commerce, and the smells of foods, spices and Chinese teas.

The market, which extends for some five blocks along Decatur Street, has had structures and temporary buildings added to it over time, giving it a rather irregular pattern. It remains today as much of an institution as ever, still a thriving marketplace and a place for socialization as well.

Wrought and cast iron grillwork is by far the most popular decoration in New Orleans, not only in balconies and galleries, but in door and window grilles, gates, fences and garden furniture. Among the best known and most photographed examples is the Cornstalk Fence, surrounding the Cornstalk Fence Hotel at 915 Royal Street in the French Quarter. The intricate design of cornstalks intertwined with morning glories is set off by gate posts that rest on pumpkins and a butterfly which adorns the center of the gate itself. Although the date of construction of this fence is unknown, it is believed to have been after 1830 when the structure was built, as cast iron began to supplement wrought iron shortly after that date.

There are at least two other cornstalk fences in New Orleans, one located in the Garden District and one in Treme. The Garden District house at 1448 Fourth Street and Prytania is a lavish showplace built for Col. Robert Short in 1859. Short spared no expense to create this 5,000 square foot ostentatious home with its 16-foot ceilings and eleven coal-burning fireplaces, erected on a property consisting of no less than ten city lots. The fence was ordered through a catalogue from Philadelphia.

Some of the city's early iron work, hand wrought or hammered using forges and anvils, was manufactured in New Orleans by black, German and Irish craftsmen. Still other examples came from the North but most of the more intricate designs were imported from Spain. There is little carbon in Spanish iron and it has remained quite resistant to rust. Cast iron, which is poured into molds and allowed to harden, came into use about 1830 and is usually painted because it rusts more easily than its forged cousin.

Wrought iron was used primarily for railings and supports, while cast iron lent itself more easily to intricate designs. Cast lace work designs are often seen gracing entire fronts and sides of corner buildings. Many of the designs used include fleur-de-lis, flowers, hearts, arrows, or family crests and monograms.

In addition to adorning homes of the living, ironwork was used to decorate many of the above-ground crypts and tombs in New Orleans cemeteries. Symbols such as crosses, lyres, angels, cupids and hearts are common sights in the cemeteries, along with the winged hourglass symbolizing the flight of time, a lamb symbolizing innocence, fruit for plenty and the weeping willow for sadness.

The Cornstalk Fence Hotel

Gallier Hall at 545 St. Charles Avenue on Lafayette Square was named for its architect, James Gallier, Sr. Construction on this magnificent building lasted from 1845 to 1850. It was used as City Hall for the English-speaking population of New Orleans, as the Cabildo served as City Hall for Creole residents. The Mayor's offices still contain the original Rococo Revival furniture.

Gallier Hall continued to serve as City Hall until 1956 and as such was the site of many major events in the city's history. Confederate President Jefferson Davis lay in state in the public parlor; Theodore Roosevelt and many other national and global leaders have been received here; and Gallier Hall was the site where Captain David Farragut of the Union Navy presided over the city's surrender in 1862.

The locale for City Hall, at the corner of Hevia and St. Charles Streets, was chosen because of its open, airy position. Ten Ionic columns located atop eighteen granite steps support a massive pediment with relief figures representing Liberty, Justice and Commerce. Another of the building's distinctive features is the Greek Revival colonnade running ninety feet in length. According to Leonard Huber's *New Orleans: A Pictorial History*, "Gallier Hall in the opinion of architectural critics is hardly surpassed in dignity and proportion by a building of the Greek Revival period in the United States." Interior renovations notwithstanding, the former City Hall remains today virtually the same as originally designed.

Gallier Hall, considered to be the finest work of its illustrious architect, still dominates the scene at Lafayette Square as it has for nearly 150 years.

⚜

The Pontalba Apartments, located on either side of Jackson Square, are the creation of Micaela Almonester de Pontalba. Her father Don Almonester y Roxas was the builder of the Cabildo, the Presbytere and the Cathedral of Saint Louis. Born in 1795 in New Orleans and educated in the Ursuline Convent, Micaela was a bright and strong-willed girl who at sixteen was wed to Celestin de Pontalba, whom his parents had affectionately dubbed "Tin-Tin." The wedding took place in the Saint Louis Cathedral; a short while later the couple left for France.

It was to be a union fraught with turmoil -- a domestic power struggle. Almost from the beginning, Micaela fought for control of the money and property left her by her father. The relationship was further strained by Micaela's increasing discomfort with her in-laws. By 1820 she had begun a lengthy legal battle that would last for decades. Micaela came into the major-

Gallier Hall

ity of her father's fortune in 1826 with the death of her mother. Her father-in-law, Baron Pontalba, was infuriated when the will legally restricted the Pontalba's from gaining control of the money. In 1834, crazed by what he perceived as a stigma on his family name, the elder Pontalba shot at Micaela, injuring her, then turned the gun on himself and committed suicide. Two years later she obtained a legal separation from his son.

Finally in 1848, the Baroness Pontalba returned to her native New Orleans and the following year began the renovation of the Place d'Armes and the construction of the noted town houses that bear her name. She turned what had been a neglected patch of ground into a beautiful European public garden. She was an ardent admirer of Andrew Jackson and renamed the transformed Place d'Armes in his honor.

There is some controversy over who actually designed the apartments, though it appears that Pontalba brought several plans with her from France. It is likely that design contributions were made by James Gallier, Jr., and possibly by her contractor, Samuel Stewart. Her expertise should come as no surprise given the influence of her father's massive construction projects. It seems the Baroness handled the entire project almost single-handedly, from supervising the design, to ordering the materials, to overseeing the actual construction. Her efforts resulted in twin structures each a block long, built in the Neoclassical style, but with more casual Creole touches.

The buildings were completed in 1851 and quickly became one of the most fashionable addresses in the city, even with, for the time, exorbitant rents. When singer Jenny Lind visited New Orleans, the Baroness gave her the use of her own apartment and the services of her personal chef.

Each building contained sixteen town houses with thick walls and folding doors which enabled rooms to be enlarged. Commercial establishments were allowed on the first floor only, and the apartments located on the second and third floors were adorned with luxurious chandeliers, marble fireplaces and beautiful rosewood furniture. Smaller rear apartments were located off the interior courtyards. The cast iron grillwork throughout the complex contained repetitions of the AP monogram for Almonester and Pontalba.

Upon Baroness Micaela Pontalba's return to France in 1851, Joseph Xavier Celestin Delfau de Pontalba sought a reconciliation with his wife, giving over to her control of all money and property. She cared for him until her death in 1874. The stunning Upper and Lower Pontalbas stand as a fitting tribute to a fascinating and remarkable woman.

⚜

During one of her many separations from her husband, Micaela Almonester de Pontalba traveled to Washington, D.C. where she met Andrew Jackson. To the horror of her French in-laws, she insisted on calling herself a "Jackson Democrat." Many years later, after returning to her native New Orleans, Micaela embarked upon a typically ambitious mission: she wanted to place a memorial to Jackson in the Place d'Armes and rename the park Jackson Square.

The Pontalba Apartments

In 1851, at a cost of $30,000, she and a group of Jackson admirers had a statue made, modeled after a sculpture done by Clark Mills. Although three statues -- the one in New Orleans, one in Washington, DC and another in Nashville, Tennessee -- were made from the original mold, as such, it is the oldest bronze equestrian representation in the country. This work weighs more than ten tons and amazingly, all this weight is supported by the two slender hind legs of the rearing horse. The statue has withstood hurricanes, ceremonial cannon shots and all manner of rumbling heavy vehicles. The streets surrounding the square are now blocked off to traffic.

The old military parade ground now called Jackson Square was landscaped by Baroness Pontalba and included walkways and hedgerows. The Square now serves as an unofficial gallery for the city's artists, who display their work during the day along its iron fence. Between them, Don Almonester and his daughter, the Baroness Micaela de Pontalba, created a striking ensemble of structures: the imposing Cathedral flanked by the Cabildo and the Presbytere, and the Pontalba buildings facing each other on either side of the square. Observing this scene on a misty morning, it is not difficult to imagine General Jackson riding by, tipping his hat to the city, or perhaps to the Baroness herself.

The house at 1239 First Street in the New Orleans Garden District is one of several owned by writer Anne Rice and poet and painter Stan Rice. It is a popular spot for tourists hoping to catch a glimpse of the famous author of *Interview With the Vampire* and many other noted novels. The home is typical of the New Orleans interpretation of the Classical style, with ornate Italianate touches, and is distinctive in part because of the double galleries with Ionic and Corinthian columns above flanked by square corner pilasters.

The contract for the original mansion was signed on January 3, 1857 by the owner, Albert Hamilton Brevard and carried the price of $13,000. James Calrow was the architect and Charles Price, one of the city's more eminent contractors, was the builder. The house was built on a lot that was half a square, extending all the way to Camp Street. Though complex and highly decorative in design, the perimeter fence was one of the patented designs that some feel is a distant ancestor of today's chain link fences. Its rose pattern gave birth to a name for the property -- "Rosegate."

Elaborate carved mahogany is found throughout the house, on door and window frames and the grand staircase. The ceilings were ornamented with intricate plaster medallions. The mantels atop the fireplaces at either end of the double parlor on the second floor are unusual in their varied design; a different season -- one Spring, one Fall -- is illustrated in marble. The gardens are spectacular and display color from early spring through autumn with a variety of flora including camellias, azaleas, a giant bougainvillea, shrimp plants and Confederate jasmine.

Brevard died after living in the house only two years. In 1869 his daughter sold it to Emory Clapp. Clapp was engaged to be married, and added his own touches to the house, including imported rosewood mirrors and double galleries with the same rose-embellished grillwork as the facade.

After Mrs. Clapp's death in 1934, the house was purchased by Mrs. Frank Brostrom. Federal Judge and Mrs. John Minor Wisdom bought the property in 1947 and Mr. and Mrs. John A. Mmahat purchased the house in 1972. A plaque on the rose fence recognizing the house's architectural and historical significance was awarded by the Orleans Parish Landmarks Commission whose seal is based on the coat of arms of Jean Baptist Le Moyne, Sieur de Bienville, founder of New Orleans.

The Anne Rice House

"Steamboat a-coming!" In the early days of shipping this call was common and brought the crews of the Port of New Orleans to life. The Mississippi River was the lifeblood of Louisiana; fur trappers, traders, mercantile establishments and livestock and cotton farmers all utilized this artery that connected them to New Orleans and other more exotic ports.

A cargo of 15,000 bear and deer hides was shipped down the Mississippi in 1705. From that time, canoes and flat boats gave way to steamboats, and finally to the massive supertankers of today. In the period following the Civil War, the Port of New Orleans, which takes up a 17-mile long strip of the Mississippi riverbank, grew to be the largest port in the world, a distinction it holds today in terms of waterborne tonnage passing through.

In 1884 the city marked the one hundredth anniversary of shipping the first bale of cotton to Europe, and dubbed it a "world's fair."

In addition to pickup and delivery of cargo, boats navigating through New Orleans carried passengers and mail to areas up and down the Mississippi River. Huge levees have since been built to protect the city from flooding, as much of it lies near sea level. Passing ships loom large and appear to float on the horizon. More than 5,000 ships a year visit the port carrying products including grain, machinery, crude oil and coffee from all parts of the globe.

Construction of the U.S. Customs House at 423 Canal Street began in 1849 with the laying of the cornerstone on the former site of Fort San Louis. A young Army engineer, the future General P.G.T. Beauregard was in charge of the project. Among the dignitaries attending the groundbreaking for the historic building was Henry Clay. By 1856 the Customs House was occupied in part, but work was delayed during the Civil War and the building served as Union headquarters under General Butler until after 1862. Further work on the structure was discontinued after 1881 and it was considered complete in 1884.

The massive building occupies the block bounded by Decatur, Iberville, North Peters and Canal Streets, and is said to have the finest Greek Revival interior in America.

In the magnificent Marble Hall shown here, which measures 125 feet by 95 feet, a glass ceiling is supported by fourteen Corinthian columns, each 58 feet high. While the interior is done in the Greek Revival style, the exterior of the building is modified Egyptian. The cornerstone side of the building sank into the swampy New Orleans soil about thirty inches and today the building rests upon deeply anchored cypress pilings. At one time the Customs House was used as a Federal prison; it also housed the city police for a time. During Reconstruction, it was the site of many riots.

The inset drawings depict the faces of Mercury, Roman god of commerce, and Luna, goddess of the moon, which are carved into the capitals of the columns in Marble Hall. Luna represents New Orleans, as the city is shaped like a crescent or quarter moon.

⚜

Voodoo queen Marie Laveau (1794?-1881) is reportedly buried in her family gravesite in St. Louis Cemetery I. The tomb bears the inscription: "Marie Philome Glapion, deceased June 11, 1897." Her daughter, Marie II, who carried on the voodoo rites after her mother's death, is thought to be buried in St. Louis Cemetery II in a crypt marked "Marie Laveau." Although records are unclear and rumors abound about which Marie is buried where, believers and followers of Marie Laveau continue to seek help from her, and bring to the sites food, money and flowers. To seek aid, according to legend, one must turn around three times and mark a cross on the stone with red brick.

For fifty years, from 1830 to 1880, the undisputed queen of voodoo lived in a house at 1020 St. Ann Street and conducted rituals in her backyard. Born a free woman of color about 1794, Marie Laveau worked as a hair-

The United States Custom House

dresser to wealthy white and Creole women of New Orleans. During that time, she became involved in the practice of Voodoo, a term derived from the name Vodun, a god or spirit. It is the national folk religion of Haiti and was probably brought to the United States in the early nineteenth century by African slaves imported from the island. The spirit or power in voodoo resides in the python and is communicated through a male priest or 'hounger' or a female 'mambo.' Followers of Marie Laveau believed her magic could bring them luck in money or love, could cure illness and impotency, and could bring tragedy to their enemies. Ironically, Marie was a devout Catholic and added the Catholic elements of statues, incense and holy water to her voodoo ceremonies.

Her daughter, Marie Glapion, or Marie II, so closely identified with her mother that she had little identity of her own. Although she carried on in her mother's footsteps as voodoo queen, the practice of voodoo diminished after the first Marie's death in 1881.

Visitors to New Orleans today are not encouraged to visit the cemeteries alone. Though picturesque and seemingly peaceful, they may shelter vandals. One should instead pay a visit to the Voodoo Museum at 724 Dumaine Street which houses displays depicting the history and rituals of voodoo from its beginnings to the present.

As for Marie Laveau, some legends hold that she never really died, but that her soul transmigrated into that of a large black crow. Both Maries are said to haunt the city and on St. John's Eve, June 23, an important date in the voodoo calendar, the shadowy figure of a woman has been seen on St. John's Bayou.

Sindsley

A piece of New Orleans and Mississippi River history has been preserved through the daily excursions available on the steamboat paddlewheelers such as the *Creole Queen, Cajun Queen, Cotton Blossom* and the one pictured here, the *Natchez*. The *Natchez*, built in 1975, is an authentic steamboat copied from two 1880s packets, the *Virginia* and the *Judson*, and is docked at the Toulouse Street Wharf at Jackson Square near the Jackson Brewery in the French Quarter. Three times a day the *Natchez* and her 35 crew members leave the dock, taking 500-800 passengers on a two-hour journey back in time. The boat travels at a leisurely seven miles per hour, propelled solely by the paddlewheel, which weighs 26 tons.

The *Natchez*, owned by the New Orleans Steamboat Company, is the latest in a line of steamboats with that name. The first *Natchez* riverboat, and six others after that, were owned by veteran riverboat captain Thomas P. Leathers. A feisty, sometimes belligerent, independent man, Leathers was in love with the city of Natchez, Mississippi and he named seven boats in honor of that city. The boat's name is a familiar one in the area; Natchez, Chickasaw, and Choctaw Indians were the first inhabitants of the territory that would become Louisiana.

Although Captain Leathers was difficult to deal with, tradesmen and others who depended on the riverboats to transport their cotton, tobacco, sugar cane, hemp and animal skins to New Orleans for distribution to other ports knew that Leathers was a conscientious and skillful captain, with a concern for the safety of his passengers and cargo. In 1870 Leathers, in *Natchez VI*, raced down the Mississippi from St. Louis to New Orleans against his rival, steamboat captain John W. Cannon in the *Robert E. Lee*. Although the *Robert E. Lee* made the best time overall, *Natchez* backers cried "foul" over the *Robert E. Lee*'s attaching to a barge and refueling in mid-river. To this day, *Natchez* historians insist that no *Natchez* has ever lost a riverboat race.

Another famous Captain, Samuel Clemens, later to become author Mark Twain, traveled to the port of New Orleans as a riverboat pilot. Mark Twain devoted ten delightful chapters in *Life on the Mississippi* to his experiences on the river and in New Orleans from 1857 to 1861.

The *Natchez* represents a day when hundreds of shallow-draft riverboats plied the waters of the Mississippi, hauling vast quantities of cotton, sugar, sugar cane, and other valuable commodities. Paddleboats were a favored mode of travel, and passengers crowded the docks in anticipation of a comfortable and entertaining trip. Saloons were hung with velvet ornamentations and orchestras and dance floors awaited the guests who slept in cabins, not numbered, but named for states of the union, hence the term "stateroom." The paddlewheelers of yesteryear, once the main source of commerce through the Port of New Orleans, now attract tourists by the thousands, who wish to experience, if only briefly, a touch of times past.

⚜

Rayne Memorial Methodist Church at 3900 St. Charles Avenue, was established in 1858 and the present building was erected in 1874. It is of red brick construction in the Gothic Revival perpendicular style. The architect was Charles Lewis Hillger who designed a number of protestant churches in the period following the Civil War. It is a fine example of ecclesiastical architecture of the late 1800s.

The carved brickwork was done by craftsmen who worked in New Orleans from around 1850 to 1880 and then moved on, leaving Rayne Memorial as one of the best examples of their work. The building was named by one of the church's donors, Robert W. Rayne, in memory of his son William who was killed at Chancellorsville.

Rayne Memorial Methodist Church

The Columns Hotel at 3811 St. Charles Street was built in 1883 for cigar merchant Simon Hernsheim. It was one of a number of homes in the Garden District designed by architect Thomas Sully, who took pains to create interiors and exteriors that were tailored to each client. Hernsheim, a native New Orleanian, was a self-made man; his company, S. Hernsheim Bros., had a monopoly on the tobacco trade and he wished to have a home that would proclaim his success to the world.

Sully's designs were extravagant and massive, and the Hernsheim home was no exception. Built on a grand scale, the structure has a four-story tower on the front, with decorative moldings at each level and a large covered gallery at the top. After a hurricane damaged the home in 1915, the Tuscan galleries to one side of the tower were replaced with irregularly spaced columns, from which the structure got its current name.

The interior of the Hernsheim home was flamboyant as well, with a columned parlor and a high degree of ornamentation in the ceilings and wall moldings. In the late 1880s gaudiness and display of opulence were the norm in New Orleans; the residence at 3811 St. Charles was rarely equaled in either excess.

When the death of his wife and the marriage of his daughter left the mansion empty, Hernsheim grew despondent and committed suicide in 1898. The home was purchased by Clementia Hubbard Norman who sold it in 1914 to Hubbard Moylen Field. The home was used as a genteel boarding house until 1953 when owner Richard Baumbach began operating it as the Columns Hotel. Much of the interior has been restored by the current owner and visitors can see firsthand a fine example of the spirit of 1890s New Orleans.

⚜

Gibson Hall, located at 6823 St. Charles Avenue on the beautiful campus of Tulane University, was built in 1893-94. Architects Benjamin Morgan Harrod and Paul Andry designed the massive structure using elements typical of late Victorian buildings. The facade is enhanced by the rhythmic repetition of Romanesque arched doors and windows. The building's plan won a national award which resulted in a commission to design the additional original campus buildings.

The educational institution itself was originally founded in 1834, sixty years prior to establishment of this campus. It evolved from the Medical College of Louisiana, broadened its scope and, after being chartered by the state, became the University of Louisiana. In 1884 the facility was renamed

The Columns Hotel

Tulane University of Louisiana in honor of Paul Tulane, a major benefactor. Sophie Newcomb College was moved from its location on Washington Avenue and combined with the University sometime around 1918. As a memorial to her daughter, Josephine Louise Newcomb had made substantial endowments to the college which came to bear her daughter's name. The Newcomb College was widely known for designing avante garde and art nouveau pottery during the late 19th and early 20th centuries, some of which can be seen at the College Art Department at 60 Newcomb Place.

Many of Tulane's administrative offices are located in Gibson Hall which bears a plaque from the Orleans Parish Landmarks Commission. Tulane is one of the many higher educational institutions in New Orleans, which include Loyola University, Dillard University, Louisiana State University Medical Center, a branch of Southern University, the University of New Orleans and Xavier University.

Lindsley

In 1880 Emile Commander established a restaurant at 1403 Washington Avenue in the Garden District. The District itself, New Orleans' first large suburban area, had developed in the early 1800s as a refuge for Anglo-Saxon emigrants to a territory and city dominated by Creole culture. By the beginning of the 1880s, the city was experiencing a post war boom and Commander saw the need for a restaurant that would serve this wealthy and distinguished neighborhood.

The elaborate Victorian structure was a perfect home for Commander's venture, and here he created excellent menus and provided impeccable service which attracted gourmets from all over the globe. The tradition was carried forward first by Frank and Elinor Moran, who bought the restaurant in 1944, and subsequently by Ella and Dick Brennan who became the owners in 1969. The blending of cultures in New Orleans is evident in the combination of Creole and American dishes which are mainstays at this establishment.

The restaurant was the recipient of the James Beard Foundation award for the nation's outstanding restaurant in 1996, an honor previously bestowed on such culinary legends as New York's Le Cirque and Los Angeles' Spago.

Though the interior was renovated extensively in the 1970s, the exterior of the house retains its Victorian "gingerbread" charm. Commander's Palace continues as a gourmet landmark in a city noted for varied and extraordinary cuisine.

The Confederate Museum at 929 Camp Street is housed in a structure built in 1889 and 1890 for the collection of the Louisiana Historical Association. The nonprofit organization's collection contains pictures, paintings, weapons, uniforms, medical instruments, memorabilia and even bloodstained battleflags from the Civil War.

When Jefferson Davis, president of the Confederacy died in New Orleans his body lay in state at the Museum for 24 hours before interment. The original structure is purely Romanesque in architecture, a style still very prevalent in the post Victorian era. The portico and turret appear to be later additions as they do not appear to be part of the original design.

A sight that lends much to the ambience of New Orleans is the St. Charles Avenue Streetcar. The city's last trolley line, it is also the oldest continuously running street railway, having started with horse-drawn trolleys in 1835 which connected New Orleans with the city of Carrolton. Some of the 35 olive-green streetcars which serve on the line today date to the 1920s.

From the line's terminus on Canal Street near the French Quarter the streetcars trundle up St. Charles Avenue, through corridors of giant old oak trees and into the city's Garden District. Here stand imposing Greek Revival homes and their extravagantly landscaped gardens, fountains, statuary and gazebos. The trolley continues past the beautiful campuses of Tulane and Loyola Universities to Audubon Park. Loyola University Chapel, which is in the background, is part of the noted educational compound built by the Jesuits in 1914.

At the end of the line passengers must alight from the cars to allow the seats to be reversed and face the new "forward" direction. Part of the New Orleans Municipal Transit System, the streetcar line is a National Landmark.

⚜

In the late 19th century architect Henry Hobson Richardson developed an interpretation of Romanesque architecture so particularly his own that it was named for him. An interest in Romanesque design, which is based on medieval English and Italian styles, emerged in the mid 1800s, but was confined primarily to ecclesiastical and public buildings. Richardson was the first to significantly carry out the style in residential architecture; this was to have great influence on the New Orleans firm of Favrot & Livaudais. Several of their structures survive; one of the best examples is probably the Brown House, or Mansion, at 4717 St. Charles Avenue.

Designed for "the bull cotton king," William Perry Brown, the house caused something of a sensation. Brown had promised his bride that her new home would be the grandest on St. Charles Avenue. Even though construction began as the boom of the 1880s had been replaced by a slowing economy that stretched into the late 1890s, Brown more than fulfilled his promise. The newspaper noted the house was "to be heated throughout with hot air, each bedroom is to have an individual bath, the lighting is to be both electric and gas..." The home, completed in 1904, remained in the family until 1979.

The massive building incorporated almost every Romanesque detail; it is distinguished by rough cut stone, huge round arches, exquisite carved detail, and a general feeling of strength and durability. The medieval character was carried through to the interior with beamed ceilings and heavy wood paneling. The simplicity of this enormous form and the consistent quality of the repeating detail make the Brown House a landmark of national importance.

The Brown Mansion

The New Orleans Museum of Art was founded in 1911 and housed in a classic example of the Greek Revival architecture so popular in New Orleans. It was originally named the Delgado Museum after its founder Isaac Delgado, a local sugar broker.

Until recently, the museum was relatively small; it was, in fact, the smallest museum in America to host a showing of the Treasures of King Tutankhamen when the exhibit toured this country. NOMA has since undergone extensive renovation and expansion. Its collection is quite comprehensive and represents art from the pre-Christian era through the present. Exhibits include Western, African and Far Eastern art as well as that of pre-Columbian America.

The museum also boasts an outstanding display of period rooms containing eighteenth and nineteenth century furniture and four centuries of French paintings including works of Pierre Auguste Renoir, Claude Monet, Paul Gaugin and Edgar Degas. In 1871-72, Degas lived with relatives in New Orleans and enjoyed life here although complaining of the poor lighting in his working quarters. He wrote, "Everything delights me here." Edgar's brothers, Achille and Rene, lived and worked at the New Orleans Cotton Exchange. The Musson family, relatives of Degas' mother, lived on Esplanade Avenue, not far from the museum's location. While in New Orleans, Degas painted family portraits and a scene depicting an afternoon at the Cotton Exchange.

Other exhibits at the museum include sculpture, photography and decorative arts as well as one of the best collections of imperial Russian Faberge eggs in the country. The museum is located in City Park at the center of a traffic circle at Carrollton and Esplanade Avenues.

⚜

The Longue Vue House and Gardens at 7 Bamboo Road in Old Metairie were constructed in the 1920s and 1930s by philanthropist Edgar Bloom Stern, a New Orleans cotton broker, and his wife Edith, daughter of Julius Rosenwald, a founder of Sears. The classic Greek Revival house, known as a 'city estate,' was designed by William and Geoffrey Platt and is on the National Register of Historic Places.

Ellen Biddle Shipman, whose extraordinary designs were also showcased in the gardens of many of the country's leading families, including the Astors and the DuPonts, was dubbed by Mrs. Stern the "Dean of American Women Landscape Architects." In 1935 she began the design and construction of eight acres of elaborate gardens at Longue Vue.

The New Orleans Museum of Art

Shipman's landscape included a walled garden, an alley of camellias leading to a Greek temple, a Wild Garden of native plants which wound through forested paths, the Pan Garden, and other areas highlighted by fountains and massive oaks. In the 1960s, after the rows of camellias were heavily damaged in Hurricane Betsy, a Spanish Court, which architect William Platt based on the fourteenth-century Generalife Gardens of the Spanish Alhambra was put in their place. A new addition is the Lucy C. Roussel Discovery Garden, a place especially for children, complete with worms, rainbows and seed-planting bed. New programs will bring to life the renovated lath house, cold frames and cutting garden.

Ellen Shipman's expertise extended to the interior of the house as well, which she decorated with fine furniture and art objects from Europe and the Orient. Appropriately, the house is now a museum of decorative arts which features changing exhibits, tours, and educational activities.

The house at 1716 Prytania Street where Lillian Hellman spent many memorable visits belonged to her two maiden aunts, sisters of her father. Born in New Orleans, Hellman moved away with her family when she was ten. She returned on numerous occasions throughout her life, but her early childhood memories and visits as a teenager left indelible impressions of the city, particularly the French Quarter.

Her aunts' house, built in 1890-91, is Victorian and plain, but a solid example of the era's architecture in upper middle class neighborhoods. The mulberry tree in which she played as a child still stands in the back yard. Hellman's best known play is *The Children's Hour*, but this house is the setting for *Toys in the Attic*.

Author William Cuthbert Faulkner (1897-1962) lived in New Orleans for several years in the 1920s. The home generally referred to as the William Faulkner House is located at 624 Pirates Alley behind St. Louis Cathedral and was built in 1840. It is reported that Faulkner's novel *Soldier's Pay* was written while he lived there.

The other occupant of the Pirate's Alley house in the 1920s was William Spratling, friend to Faulkner and playwright Sherwood Anderson. Faulkner and Spratling even collaborated on a book about New Orleans artistic figures, including their friend, entitled *Sherwood Anderson and Other Famous Creoles*. Spratling, a professor of architecture at Tulane University, later moved to Taxco, Mexico where his founding of the artistic silver industry there revitalized and forever changed the history and economy of this small mining community. But he always maintained close ties to his compatriots in New Orleans.

Before moving to the residence at Pirate's Alley, Faulkner shared quarters with Sherwood Anderson in the LeMonnier mansion at 640 Royal Street and wrote in its distinctive third story oval room. Built in 1811, this brick structure of three stories was known as the city's first "skyscraper;" the fourth story was added in 1876. Another literary resident was George Washington Cable who wrote *Old Creole Days* there in 1879.

In 1988 Joseph DeSalvo and his wife Rosemary James bought the William Faulkner House at Pirate's Alley; the upper floors are used for living and guest quarters. Appropriately, on the first floor DeSalvo opened Faulkner House Books, a small, highly respected rare book shop. In addition, he has established the annual Pirate's Alley William Faulkner Creative Writing Competition.

⚜

The house at 636 St. Peter Street is another location in New Orleans with a literary history. Built in 1842, the house is only one of several lived in by playwright Tennessee Williams. Born in 1911, Tennessee Williams attended the University of Missouri and Washington University in St. Louis, receiving his bachelor's degree in 1938 from the University of Iowa.

New Orleans has found many ways to recognize its distinguished literary residents. The young man who was a fledgling playwright in 1940s New Orleans could not have forseen the honors his adopted home would eventually bestow upon him. The Tennessee Williams-New Orleans Literary Festival is held every year in early March, largely at La Petit Theatre at 616 St. Peter Street. La Petit claims honors as the oldest continuously operating

The William Faulkner House

community theatre in the United States. The Literary Festival is one of the finest of its kind.

New Orleans streetcars were named for the areas of the city to which they transported their passengers. One such location was Desire, a street lined with tenements which the streetcars visited on a regular basis. Williams wrote *A Streetcar Named Desire* while he lived on St. Peter Street, which was only a block and a half away from the "Desire's" route on Bourbon Street. The play won the New York Drama Critics Award in 1947.

Sadly, the area which inspired this namesake streetcar has fallen victim to urban decay and is no longer visited by streetcars. But the memory of its better days and the streetcar named for Desire will live on as long as lovers of great literature continue to read and perform Tennessee Williams' work.

The Tennesee Williams House

New Orleans has indeed had a rich literary history. Some locales lend themselves to description better than others, and New Orleans is certainly such a place. Printing came to Louisiana as early as 1764 with newspaper "broadsides." But early authors wrote generally scholarly works and only in French. There was no contributor of national importance associated with the city before John James Audubon, who spent a part of two winters here in 1821 and 1822 taking notes for his *Birds of America*. Walt Whitman worked on the New Orleans *Crescent* for a few months in 1848 until his younger brother's illness forced them to return home to New England.

The Civil War and the period immediately following it were dormant times, but with the publication of "Sieur George," George Washington Cable found himself hailed as a genius, so rich were his stories of Creole life. Younger contemporaries of Cable were Grace King and Kate Chopin. King, in her novels and stories, enriched American literature with the local color of New Orleans and Chopin was a novelist of national stature.

In January 1921, a group of young intellectuals, deciding that it was time for the city to break with the old traditions and become acquainted with the new, established the *Double Dealer*, a liberal magazine with very modernist tendencies. The magazine lasted another five years, publishing some of the best-known writers of the time, including some who lived in the city, such as Sherwood Anderson and William Faulkner, and others outside New Orleans, Ernest Hemingway and Thornton Wilder, for example. Local authors gathered occasionally for lunch at Arnaud's on Bienville Street in the French Quarter and at the old St. Charles Hotel.

Anderson and Faulkner often met on the benches in front of St. Louis Cathedral and could be found in animated conversation about the state of literature. Anderson advised Faulkner to go home, to write about what he knew best -- life in rural Mississippi. That sage advice resulted years later in a Nobel Prize for Literature. Anderson also had a warm relationship with Gertrude Stein who came to New Orleans because he was there. His concern and encouragement made him mentor to a whole generation of American writers.

New Orleans newspapers spawned a large number of authors in the early decades of the twentieth century, including Lafcadio Hearn, Harnett T. Kane, Hamilton Basso and Lyle Saxon. Both Lillian Hellman and Truman Capote were born in New Orleans. Capote's family moved away when he was young, but Hellman claims that, as a teenager, regular visits to the French Quarter with a maiden aunt were a major part of her education.

Tennessee Williams is perhaps the dominant figure associated with literature in New Orleans. Not only did he write his immortal *A Streetcar Named Desire* there, but it is set in the city as well. The play contains what one critic has called the greatest line in American literature: "I have always depended upon the kindness of strangers." A gem in any discussion of literary New Orleans is John Kennedy Toole, author of the novel *A Confederacy of Dunces* which won the Pulitzer Prize in 1981. Noted writer Walker Percy was a New Orleanian in the late 1950s when he wrote *The Moviegoer*. And of course, there is the indomitable Anne Rice.

The gumbo of New Orleans culture has fed the creativity of many writers, only a few of whom are touched on here. It is clear that such a diverse and intriguing city provides inspiration that is unforgettable.

Creole cuisine, a combination of French, Spanish and African cooking, evolved from the necessity of disguising the gaminess of meats kept without refrigeration in a subtropical climate. It calls for delicate sauces and subtle seasonings. Cajun cooking, on the other hand, developed on the bayou and also traces its roots to a combination of nationalities. Sausage, hot peppers and roux characterize Cajun cuisine, which is usually hotter and heartier than Creole. But whatever style is desired, a visitor to New Orleans can be sure to find it at an eatery in one of the Jackson Brewery complexes. And the food can be enjoyed in locations that overlook the Mississippi which can be viewed from inside or outside.

Jackson Brewery, also called Jax Brewery, is the large building on the riverside of Decatur at St. Peter Street. Built in 1891, it incorporates a great deal of the elegance and charm with which industrial buildings were endowed in those days. It exemplified the diversity of the French Quarter where houses, shops and factories were built side by side. The structure has since been restored and now contains a complex of shops and eateries. Although the famous brew is no longer made here, the sign proclaiming "Home of Jax Beer" still sits atop the building .

The Jackson Brewery complex is connected to a sister property, the Jackson Brewery Millhouse, which is another restored structure housing restaurants and boutiques. A block along Canal Street is the Marketplace, which is the third festival marketplace belonging to the Jackson Brewery Corporation.

Just behind the Jax Brewery is the Toulouse Street Wharf, docking point for the steamboat *Natchez*, and the Moonwalk, a wooden walkway which leads right to the river. The Moonwalk was named for former New Orleans mayor, "Moon" Landrieu and is one of the best places to relax on a bench, be serenaded by street musicians and contemplate life on the mighty Mississippi.

⚜

The Louise S. McGehee School, founded in 1912, has occupied the house at 2343 Prytania Street since 1929. James Freret designed the magnificent structure which was built in 1872 for sugar plantation heir Brandish Johnson. Construction of the house came during the post bellum rebirth of grand style in the Garden District. The finest Renaissance architectural detail is evident in the facade which has four pairs of fluted Corinthian columns rising to the top of the first floor, six decorated windows on the second floor, and an elaborately ornamented cupola in the center of the third. The interior is marked

The Jackson Brewery

The Louise S. McGehee School

by high ceilings and intricately detailed moldings and decoration. But the centerpiece is a grand mahogany-railed staircase which sweeps upward in a magnificent spiral from the marble floor of the entrance hall toward a stained glass skylight. The stairway is remarkable not only for its beauty but for its extraordinary engineering. The house is surrounded by a beautiful landscape which includes numerous azaleas and many stately magnolias, the largest of which has been called the grandest specimen of its type.

The McGehee School was founded as an independent, nonsectarian college preparatory day school for girls. Several private schools have been located the Garden District over the last two centuries. The School carries on a long tradition which has revered fine education for generations.

Eindsley

Temple Sinai at 6221 St. Charles Avenue, founded in 1872, was the first Reformed Jewish congregation in New Orleans. The present structure was built in 1928. The auditorium which seats 1000 is a modern interpretation of the Byzantine architecture of Constantinople; a domed roof surmounts it. In the new addition there is an original stained glass window by renowned artist Ida Kohlmeyer.

Over the years the Temple has been noted for a number of firsts, demonstrating its ecumenism and compassion in the process. In 1891 and 1892 the former Temple Sinai offered its facilities to a Roman Catholic congregation that had been burned out of its own church building. In 1949 it provided a place for Ralph Bunch to speak when all other auditoriums that could accommodate a large crowd were segregated. The first women rabbis in the United States were employed here, and the Temple was the first to have its rabbi invited, in 1988, to a papal coronation.

This New Orleans version of the plantation home "Tara" from Margaret Mitchell's *Gone With the Wind* was designed in 1941 by architect Andrew M. Lockett. Built as a private home for George Palmer and his family, the facade is not a true replica, as the original "Tara" had four windows on the second floor and a full two-story wing on the left. The New Orleans structure has five second-story windows and a glass-enclosed porch over the porte cochere.

The home has another notable feature, one that is far removed from the gentility of the Southern Plantation. A bomb shelter designed to keep Palmer's family in comfort for at least 72 hours was added in 1955 and is still part of the gardens to the side of the house.

The likeness of the home to that designed for the movie is remarkable however, and it is reported that Thomas Mitchell, the actor who played Gerald O'Hara in the film, once knocked on the door and said, "I believe I live here."

A must-see, and hear, for jazz lovers in New Orleans is Preservation Hall at 726 St. Peter Street, where visitors are entertained nightly by both local and visiting bands and performers. Seating is limited in this popular night spot, which is in a building some two centuries old. A few hard benches are available; many fans stand just to be entertained by the Preservation Hall Jazz Band, playing what is truly *American* music.

Jazz, this most individual, intimate musical form, emerged in New Orleans, and traces its roots to African tribal dances and early freed black street vendors' chants. Along with constitutional freedom for the blacks in New Orleans came the freedom to express themselves in an ever-emerging musical form. Gourds, wooden whistles and cigar-box stringed instruments gave way to cornets, trombones, banjos and violins.

The music that developed was full of twists and turns and long runs of extensive melodic repetition, which was then echoed and improvised upon by the accompanying musicians. The jazz scene in New Orleans spawned such greats as Buddy Bolden, Jelly Roll Morton and the legendary Louis "Satchmo" Armstrong. When asked to define jazz, Armstrong was said to have replied, "If you gotta ask, you'll never know."

In the 1970s a modest celebration of New Orleans' musical heritage began. This annual event, dubbed "Jazzfest," has grown into a seven-day festival of impressive proportions.

All year round, whatever classic genre is preferred, be it ragtime or Dixieland, hot or cool, jazz or blues, Preservation Hall has it all.

⚜

The Louisiana Superdome holds the Guiness World Record as the largest clear-span steel structure in the world. Held together by its 9.7 acre, 680-foot-diameter roof, the Superdome is a marvel of engineering technology and ingenuity.

In the 1960s, New Orleans businessman Dave Dixon started the ball rolling toward construction of the Superdome in hopes of attracting a professional football franchise to the city. Construction began in August, 1971 and the Superdome officially opened in August, 1975, at a cost of $163 million. Architect Buster Curtis credits much of the success of the design to technological advances in computers and prestressed pilings.

A dramatic moment during the dome's construction occurred on June 12, 1973, when the scaffolding was removed, piece by piece, proving that the roof could stand without auxiliary support. The key feature in the roof construction is the series of overlapping triangles, called a "lamella" construc-

Preservation Hall

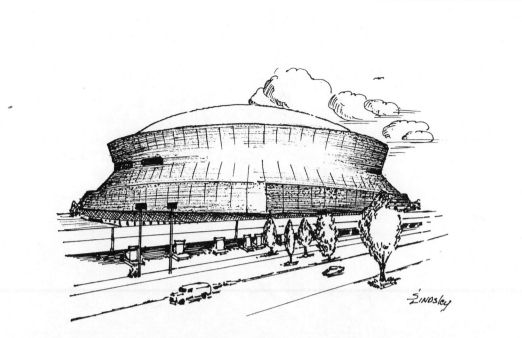

tion, which stabilizes against downward forces. A 75-ton gondola which hangs from the center of the roof provides not only protection but added stability. The drainage system combined with the construction of the foundation, the floating action of the roof tension ring and various wind braces, all contribute to the Superdome's overall structural integrity.

The Superdome's versatility is incredible. With the touch of a button, the moveable stands can be made to form configurations suitable for football, basketball, gymnastics, ice shows or any of a multitude of stadium events. The telescoping stands make it possible for the dome to seat from 14,000 for a basketball game to 87,000 for convention-sized activities. The base of the floor is concrete and, depending on the event, is covered with a wood floor, ice for ice shows and hockey games, concert stages, tons of dirt or artificial turf. A climate control system maintains the Superdome's temperature at an even 72 degrees.

Home to the New Orleans Saints football team, the Superdome is also the site of the annual Sugar Bowl Classic as well as other major sporting events. It has been the location of five NFL Superbowl games, more than any other single location, including Superbowl XXXI in 1997. The dome can accommodate several events at one time and boasts a fast "turnaround time" for multiple events during the weekends. Among the records held by the Superdome is the audience of 87,500 for the Rolling Stones concert in 1981, the largest audience for an indoor concert.

The Superdome, a large and impressive structure, has brought a variety of very special moments to the city and a new life to an area of New Orleans that was once dominated by warehouses and railroad yards.

Audubon Park, which borders the Mississippi River between Exposition Boulevard, Walnut Street and St. Charles Avenue across from Tulane and Loyola Universities, was named for bird and wildlife artist John James Audubon. The park was developed during the 1870s on the site of Etienne deBore's plantation, cradle of the sugar cane industry after deBore developed a process for refining sugar. In 1884, the World's Industrial and Cotton Exhibition was held here. Visitors were amazed by the display of both indoor and outdoor electric lighting. The park features lagoons, fountains, bicycle trails and a miniature train as well as picnic areas, tennis courts, a swimming pool and an 18-hole golf course.

Audubon Park Zoo, one of the nation's preeminent zoos, is just south of the park at 6500 Magazine Street and features 58 acres containing over 2,000 native and exotic animals and birds. Visitors can experience the lushness of tropical vegetation while observing avian species, and can travel the world of nature in the recreated habitats of the African Savanna, Australian Outback, Asian Domain and the World of Primates. Grasslands of the World can be toured on foot or via guided tour on the Mombasa Tram.

Animals native to Louisiana such as nutria, black bear, otters and rare white alligators can be seen in the Louisiana Swamp Exhibit, while links to ancient species are explored through Pathways to the Past. Live animal demonstrations, a petting zoo and an interactive butterfly exhibit are also popular features. This fine facility not only entertains visitors, but educates them about the real dangers of animal extinction due to worldwide habitat destruction.

What city does not have its characters -- those people whose often quirky individualities endear them to business people, residents and visitors alike? One such well-known personage who has graced Jackson Square in the French Quarter for more than fifty years is Ruthie, the Duck Lady. A native of the French Quarter, Ruthie got her first duck when she was nine. She named that first duck "Miss Crony," a name she has used for her pets many times since then.

Over the years, Ruthie was often seen wheeling about the Quarter on roller skates, decked out in colorful style, usually with a duck or two not far behind. The roller skates have since been put up, but Ruthie still appears in her usual eccentric attire, willing to talk to just about anyone who will listen. Though her ducks are pets, they're not exactly what one would term well-trained, as evidenced by their ability to tie up traffic as they wait for Ruthie to emerge from one of her many stopping places.

The artist counts Ruthie among his dear friends and used her as the subject of a prize-winning Mardi Gras poster. "The French Quarter needs and breeds characters like the Duck Lady and probably would have invented her had she not evolved on her own."

Lindsky

One of the top five aquariums in the United States, the Aquarium of the Americas is located on the Mississippi River at Canal Street. It was built in 1988 and is a two-story structure housing over 6,000 specimens representing 500 species of marine life found throughout the world. Among the exhibits that add to the Aquarium's popularity are the 180-pound tarpon which is the largest in captivity, and the acrylic walk-through tunnel in the Caribbean Reef exhibit.

An Amazon exhibit replicates the rain forest, complete with waterfalls and red-bellied piranhas. Visitors can observe penguins and sharks in the Living Water exhibit; a "touch pool" is a favorite with children. A Louisiana display features white alligators and other species native to the swamps and bayous of the southeast. Aquatic animals are featured throughout the complex in tanks that hold as much as one-half million gallons of water.

The Aquarium is a prominent feature of the New Orleans Waterfront, located amidst the 16-acre Woldenberg Riverfront Park. Many visitors and residents make the journey to the aquarium on the John James Audubon Aquarium/Zoo Cruise, which departs from Audubon Landing.

Mardi Gras - the last rite of the New Orleans Carnival season, is officially celebrated on Shrove Tuesday which is the day before Ash Wednesday, the beginning of Lent on the Christian Calendar. On that day, the last in the two-week celebration that has come to be known as Mardi Gras, two parades are held - Rex, King of Carnival (pictured), and Comus, God of Revelry. Rex, official King for the day, leads his parade down Canal Street while his Queen waits on the reviewing stand. The legendary Zulu Krewe also enlivens Canal Street.

It is said that there are only two seasons in New Orleans - Carnival and after-Carnival. Although preparations go on all year, Carnival season begins January 6 with elaborate private balls and celebrations, and continues through Ash Wednesday, the final two weeks being the most festive. Carnival productions and parades are in the hands of private organizations, called "krewes," each presided over by a specially selected King and Queen. The first "krewe" was the "Mystick Krewe of Comus," which appeared in 1857, though celebrations by masked students go back to 1827.

In 1872, the celebrations were attended by Alexis Alexandrovich Romanov, then a twenty-two-year-old Russian Grand Duke, who was destined to secure his place in history as the last Tsar of Russia. In an effort to stage a special celebration, the city crowned a new King - Rex, King of Carnival, Lord of Misrule.

The celebration's origins are probably rooted in the pagan rites of Spring, which over the centuries have adapted to the theme of celebrating the flesh before having to deny one's pleasures during Lent. In Paris, Mardi Gras was a fertility celebration, and as late as the 19th century a fatted ox was paraded through the streets on Shrove Tuesday in imitation of a Roman sacrificial procession. Whatever the Carnival's beginnings, it remains a genuine New Orleans festival, attended by visitors, but primarily staged for the enjoyment and delight of local revelers.

⚜

Coffee is considered a staple in New Orleans, and one of its most notable homes is the Cafe du Monde at the corner of Decatur and St. Ann Streets. This open-air pavilion downriver from Washington Artillery Park has been in the same location for over one hundred years and is considered *the* place for cafe au lait and beignets. It was rebuilt in 1975 from a building that was said to have been erected in 1813.

To a native New Orleanian, coffee is as important as life itself; it should be "as pure as an angel, strong as love, black as the Devil and hot as Hell."

Rex - King of Carnival

Most New Orleans coffee contains chicory -- ten percent or more -- and locals swear that New Orleans coffee is better than any in the world.

Many love the creamy richness of Cafe du Monde's cafe au lait, half coffee, half milk, not boiled together but mixed just before drinking. Whether a patron is starting their day, ending it, or just trying to get through it, Cafe du Monde is there to help.

A visit to Cafe du Monde would not be complete without an order of beignets, a type of French doughnut that is heavily coated in powdered sugar. Like potato chips, it is said that "nobody can eat just one," and they are nearly impossible to eat neatly. A local tradition says that if you have coffee and beignets here, you will always come back to New Orleans.

BIBLIOGRAPHY

For more information about the history of New Orleans, contact the Historic New Orleans Collection or consult your local library. Below is a sampling of resources.

Arrigo, Joseph A. *The French Quarter & Other New Orleans Scenes*. Gretna: Pelican Publishing Company. 1976.

Boorstin, Daniel J. et al, ed. *Visiting Our Past: America's Historylands*. Washington, DC: The National Geographic Society. 1977.

Bruce, Curt. *Great Houses of New Orleans*. New York: Knopf. 1977.

Curtis, Nathaniel Cortlandt. *New Orleans, Its Old Houses, Shops and Public Buildings*. Philadelphia & London: J. B. Lippincott Company. 1933.

Da Costa, Beverly, ed. *Great Historic Places - An American Heritage Guide*. New York: American Heritage Publishing Co.

Huber, Leonard V. *Landmarks of New Orleans*. Louisiana Landmarks Society and Orleans Parish Landmarks Commission. 1984.

King, Grace. *New Orleans, The Place and the People*. New York: The MacMillan Company. 1934.

Kirk, Susan Lauxman and Smith, Helen Michel. *The Architecture of St. Charles Avenue*. Gretna: Pelican Publishing Company. 1977.

Muse, Vance. *Old New Orleans*. Oxmoor House. c. 1988.

Robinson, Lura. *It's An Old New Orleans Custom*. New York: Vanguard Press. 1948.

Schlesinger, Dorothy et al, ed. *New Orleans Architecture*, Vol. VII. Gretna: Pelican Publishing Company. 1989.

Starr, S. Frederick. *Southern Comfort - The Garden District of New Orleans, 1800-1900*. Cambridge, Mass.: The M.I.T. Press. 1989.